THE MOST FABULOUS JEWELS IN THE WORLD

THE MOST FABULOUS JEWELS IN THE WORLD

Photograph: Fadil Berisha, New York.

GRAFF

FAB
THE

BLE

There are many different kinds of fable. One of the most enduring – going back to the dawn of human history – is the tale of transformation from poor boy to prince. The story of Graff is a glittering fable of our times: a fabulous transition from humble beginnings to the King of Diamonds; the jeweller of choice for kings and queens, heads of state, red-carpet celebrities and the richest people on the 21st-century planet; the elegant, slightly mysterious *diamantaire* and major art collector, who sails on his yacht or flies in his private plane to meet his clients – with something wonderful in his pocket which he has just created from a handful of glittering diamonds.

Graff, the company known for selling the most fabulous jewels in the world, is the creation of one man.

Laurence Graff started what has become an international jewellery empire nearly half a century ago with just one ring set with 33 very small diamonds to create the biggest flash he could.

This tale starts in the impoverished East End of London, where the young Laurence Graff was apprenticed at the age of fifteen to Schindler's workshop, twelve flights up in Hatton Garden. Graff learnt his craft at day-release classes at the Central School of Arts and Crafts, and went out to get sandwiches for the crew at

DWIN

BRANCHES.
MANCHESTER.
SOUTHAMPTON.
HULL.
EDINBURGH.
BELFAST.

MANUFACTURERS
OF
ELECTRO-PLATE CUTLERY,
GOLD & SILVERWARE.

TRADE *Embassy* REG^D MARK

A GUARANTEE OF QUALITY

**LARGEST BUYERS
OF GOLD & COINS
TOP PRICES**

TOP PRICES FOR GOLD & COINS
N. KAYMAN 1ST FLOOR

N. KAYMAN
WHOLESALE
JEWELLER

HARRY LEWIS & SON
DIAMOND MOUNTERS.
FIRST FLOOR

ZOX M'F'G C^O
3rd Floor

Embassy
GLADWIN LTD.
& F. BALLARD & C^O

THE FABLE

work. After three months he was called in and told he would never make the grade, and he lost his job.

Eventually, Graff found another job at Segal & Co., where he began to be taught how to make jewellery by Mr Cant, an experienced craftsman. He started to learn how to repair rings, how to solder and shape them and how to make small pieces of jewellery. By the time he was seventeen, he considered himself a jeweller and, in his free time, made very small Stars of David at a bench in his parents' house and sold them to friends of the family.

Then Segal & Co. went out of business and Graff, now eighteen, got another job where he met an older jeweller called Frank Nicholls. Graff persuaded Nicholls that they should set up in business together. They formed a partnership, found a workshop just big enough for two benches, and began to repair jewellery for the big jewellery chains, offering a 24-hour service for rings, putting on new claws and soldering new half-shanks.

Eventually, Graff and his partner started to make copies of Victorian jewellery, as well as repair it, and the business grew. Graff met an engraver who would pierce the metal shanks to make the rings look more Victorian. These sold so well he decided that it was time to get a bigger workshop. Nicholls would make the pieces and Graff would do the selling. This went well at first, but they ended up owing £3,000 to their suppliers of gold and gemstones. Facing bankruptcy, Graff, now 22,

Left: Hatton Garden at the time Laurence Graff started his apprenticeship.

THE FABLE

took over the business and the debts. He went to the suppliers and persuaded them to give him more credit – and paid back every penny within six months.

Then he took the first steps on the long road to selling jewels worth millions. He started to make samples of semi-precious rings using citrines and amethysts set in the then fashionable Victorian style with engraved and pierced bezels, shanks and claws. The engraver he used suggested he take these rings round the antique shops and that is when Graff says he learned about marketing and that you must always have samples to show, so that you can always be ready to take orders. He travelled round Britain with his samples and sold rings for about £4. Not content with this growing business, he decided to upgrade his rings set with semi-precious stones into rings set with diamonds, because he thought it a good idea to try to sell something for £50. He had seen diamonds set into half hoops and thought they looked rather pleasing.

Before Segal's had gone out of business, Graff had met a diamond dealer called Mr Rabinowitz, who he persuaded to advance him 33 small diamonds, all of which he used to make into his first diamond hoop. It cost him £60. This ring was really well made, remembers Graff. It was fabulous – there was a big flash of diamonds and underneath was beautifully engraved piercing. He sold the ring to a jeweller in Blackpool for £100. When Graff got back to London, the telephone rang in his tiny office and the owner of the Blackpool shop told

left
Laurence Graff inspecting a ballerina ring, so-called due to the undulating setting reminiscent of a ballerina's tutu.

below left
Anne-Marie Graff

below
The documentation from Hambros Bank announcing the flotation of the company in 1973. The company was privatised in 1976 and has remained so ever since.

Above: Graff's shop in Hatton Garden opened in 1962. It was the first retail outlet to open in what had traditionally been a manufacturing and wholesale district.

Top right: Laurence Graff's million-pound jewelled hair creation, early 1970s.

Right: At an early trade show in New York.

him he had sold the ring and wanted another one immediately. At first Graff found it unbelievable that he had sold £200 worth of rings overnight. Now, nearly 50 years later, one Graff diamond ring will sell for millions.

Graff went back to Mr Rabinowitz, managed to extend his credit and thought of other ways to create unique rings that everybody would want – variants on the big flash of stones. First, he took one diamond and put six stones around it, then twelve stones around that to create a nineteen-stone cluster. After making all-diamond rings, he started working with diamonds and emeralds, diamonds and rubies, diamonds and sapphires. And then he made a candy-striped collection.

Graff soon found himself in the diamond business. He started to be fascinated by these mysterious stones from the earth's core, looking at them closely, studying the small round diamonds or melees. He began to be able to see right into their depths to understand their purity and the way they had been cut. He also saw that he had found his true profession. Without realising it, he was becoming a real self-taught gemmologist and he felt that this was what he had been born to do.

It wasn't long before Graff started using ever larger stones of three and four carats and began to make a name for himself as an original designer. Still travelling around the country with samples, he decided to open his own retail store to sell his designs. This he did in 1962, with La Petite Bijouterie in Lancaster Gate. That same year he also opened Laurence Graff (Jewellery Creations) in Hatton Garden, London's diamond centre. This was the first retail store in what had traditionally been solely a wholesale and workshop quarter. The front part of the store was the shop, while Graff worked on his designs in the back, buying diamonds and precious stones that he would send out to freelance workshops in the area to be made up.

In 1966, aged just 28, his design talents were recognised by the industry when he won the prestigious Diamond International Award, competing against 300-plus designers from 23 countries. His winning design was an amethyst, emerald and diamond bracelet with the stones typically clustered together to obtain the maximum effect.

But Graff was frustrated. He felt the next step would be to sell his designs to the top jewellers of the time, but they were not interested. The eager young designer met a wall of indifference and he had to sell his creations to a lower bracket of jewellers and to second-hand shops around the country. Graff has never claimed to be an artist, but he did – and does – create unique and interesting pieces. He wanted to make bigger and bigger pieces, but who would buy them?

Impatient to get ahead, he decided the only way to do this was to travel, taking his designs out into a wider world of opportunity and adventure.

So the young man set out on the first of his extraordinary voyages, beginning in Australia, where he travelled with his nineteen-stone clusters in a suitcase. Soon

Laurence Graff travelled all over the world with a suitcase of rings.

In San Francisco in the late 1960s.

In Tahiti with his suitcase of sample rings.

after arriving, he found a wholesaler and made him his distributor. Then he took his samples further afield around South East Asia, going first to Singapore, which he had heard about from his father who had been there during World War II.

When he arrived he asked where the centre of town was and was directed to Raffles Hotel, where planters from up-country and the Malaysian aristocracy met and socialised. He had a stroke of luck, or coincidence, one of many in his life. He walked into Robinson's, Singapore's leading department store at the time, the equivalent of Harrods but smaller. One of the managers caught sight of the young man with the sample case and hailed him as an old friend. He had been the manager of a shop in the North of England to whom Graff had sold rings. He was in the process of starting up a jewellery department at Robinson's and didn't have any stock.

Graff immediately showed him his samples, but the manager told him there weren't enough to stock a department. Graff assured him that he could go back to London immediately and return with more than enough new pieces to put on an exhibition, which he did. He remembers how exciting this adventurous phase of his life was, travelling into the unknown.

He was a young man in an exotic wonderland, a faraway place where there were a lot of very wealthy Malaysians, Indians and Chinese, all of whom really loved jewellery.

The exhibition at Robinson's attracted all the smart women from Singapore, from up-country Malaya, and other parts of South East Asia, who came to buy his 'big flashes'.

Raffles Hotel, Singapore, the crossroads of Malaysia.

THE FABLE

Early examples of Graff's jewellery design.
Above: The necklace set in 18 carat white gold was made in honour of the Queen's Silver Jubilee in 1977.

Right: The amethyst, emerald and diamond bracelet won the Diamond International Award in 1966, competing against 321 designers from 23 countries.

THE FABLE

One important early client was the young Crown Prince of Brunei's wife, now Queen of Brunei and still, with her husband the Sultan, both friends and clients of Graff.

He started to sell thousands of pounds' worth of jewels, then tens of thousands of pounds' worth. He made bigger and bigger pieces back in London, some based on traditional Malayan jewellery, and travelled back to Singapore with them. This, in essence, was the foundation of his present-day retail business. For, even though he was already a designer, a manufacturer and a wholesaler, the shop in Robinson's was, in a sense, his first shop abroad.

So important did this business become that Graff went to Singapore four and then five or six times a year, then to other parts of the Far East to put on exhibitions and to sell to both wholesalers and retailers. He went to places he had never heard of before: Sandakan, Tawau, Sabah, Brunei Darussalam, Sarawak. He went to rubber plantations, tiny Sultanates and teak plantations. Odd, remote places where a bright young man with a suitcase of 72 glittering samples was a novel and interesting sight, and was made welcome. He sold the samples only in extreme circumstances, taking orders instead. A big trip would net large orders, ten of this ring, five of that, twenty of another. From the original 72 sample rings Graff might sell 300 on one trip to be made up back in London.

Voyaging to strange and remote lands as he did, Graff was the latterday Tavernier of the jewellery business. Jean-Baptiste Tavernier was the 17th-century adventurer who

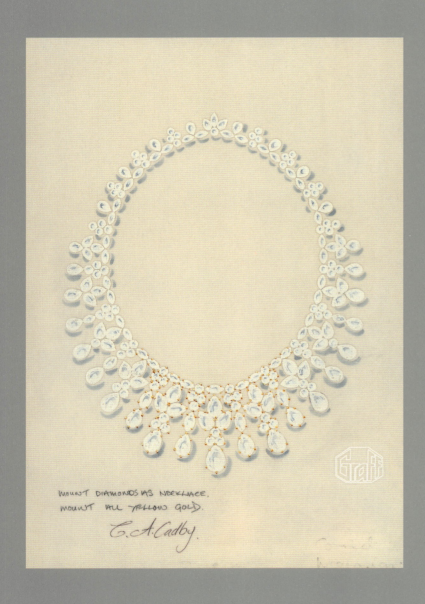 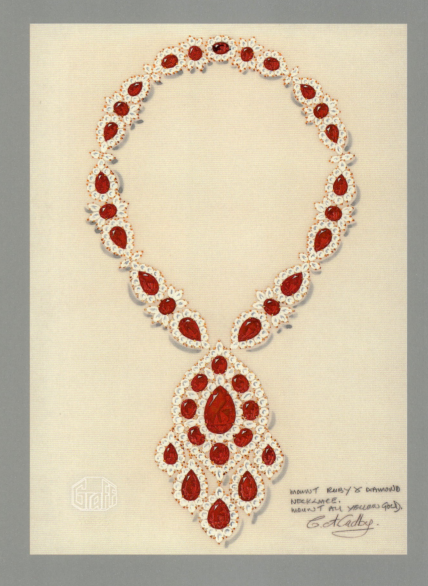

Early Graff designs, showing the increasing intricacies
of the fluid settings and stamped with the original logo of the house.

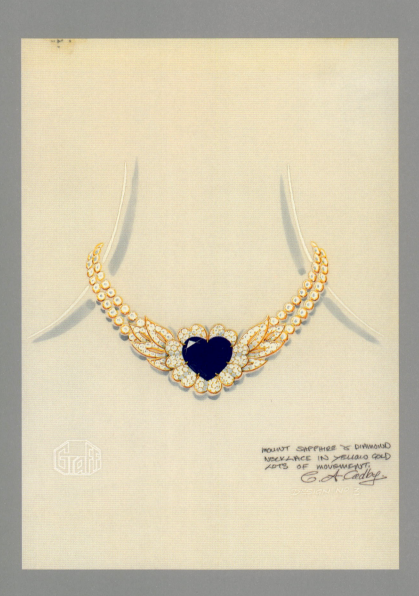

THE FABLE

went to India to look for diamonds to sell to European royalty, especially Louis XIV. Like him, Graff was truly a pioneer at a time in Asia when people would turn around and look at Europeans in the street. He must have been an interesting sight to them, a good-looking young man, well-dressed and carrying a suitcase full of gems. The Middle East was his next port of call, specifically Kuwait, where an Indian jeweller introduced him to a client who was the wife of a sheikh. Through selling a little boutique ring to the sheikha, while sitting on a carpet, he met her husband, who invited him to his palace for dinner, which was how Graff began to get to know royalty and the wealthy in the area. He was a novelty; friendly, presentable and he had a story to tell that they wanted to hear.

He decided to travel even further, from the South Pacific to the Caribbean and eventually to major European cities, always on his own, always with his case of samples, always making contacts and friends and setting up local wholesale connections. But Graff did not neglect his domestic market. He began to create unique themed stands at Earl's Court amongst other venues.

He also began to create an aura of myth and excitement around his jewels,

notably in 1970 when he designed 'Hair and Jewel', a million-dollar coiffure, using a combination of silver blonde hair and an enormous number of diamonds and

Right: A 1980s Graff advertising image.

gemstones, inspired by royal coiffures at 18th-century Versailles – a glittering variant on the big flash, the original foundation of his business and his eventual fortune.

Graff's success abroad had not gone unnoticed and, in 1973, he became the first jeweller to be presented with the Queen's Award for Enterprise for International Trade. His exports had increased more than five times in the preceding three years and over 60 per cent of the company's total output went abroad. Since that first Award, Graff has won three further awards, the latest in 2006.

By 1973 the business had grown so much, both at home and abroad, that Graff decided to take his company public, appointing Hambros Bank, which already had diamond trade connections, to act as his bankers. He was 32 and he was going public, proving what an East End boy could do. He is proud of this achievement to this day. But, being an independent entrepreneur, he quickly found that running a public company meant that he had lost control of the business he had so painstakingly built up, and that his travels in search of new business became difficult now that he was the chairman of a public company. Within four years he bought his business back and since then he has never brought in any outside shareholders, nor has he chosen to re-capitalise. Graff looks back on that four-year period and credits it with teaching him to become a sophisticated businessman.

In 1974 Graff opened a state-of-the-art retail shop in Knightsbridge, his new headquarters. He still travelled the world doing exhibitions, but at that time there was an

Above: Graff at an auction in the mid-1980s.

Top left: The Graff Diamond workshops at 16 Greville Street, Hatton Garden.

Top right: Laurence Graff with Prince Charles at a private dinner in 1976.

Left: The first major retail shop opened in 1974 on the Brompton Road.

Graff jewels, 1982

influx of Middle Eastern oil money in London, so he concentrated on welcoming his clients from all over the world, drawn to Graff by seeing his jewellery at exhibitions, in the increasingly sophisticated advertising he was doing in glossy magazines, or from buying from him during his visits to their countries. When they visited London in the summer to shop, they came to see him. His Majesty the Sultan of Brunei, who had become a faithful client during Graff's visits to his country, walked in really early on. So did many members of the Saudi Arabian and Gulf royal families and the many other Middle Eastern families he had got to know.

They treated his shop and the office behind it like their own palaces, using it to change their clothes when they bought something new to wear.

Sometimes there were so many clients in the store they were not only lounging on the settees, but perching on the tables and even sitting on the floor. They liked Graff, because he was young, had a sense of humour and had exactly what they wanted to buy. Moreover, he knew how to trade with them. He could bargain with them and he made it amusing.

The deals became even bigger and more exotic. Once Graff packed a trunk with 400 pieces of jewellery to show to a prince, who bought the lot in a single swoop. It was not uncommon for him to sell 50 watches at a time. Those were the golden years and it was better that Graff was available to his clients in his shop than travelling to meet them. Sometimes other traders would go to Saudi Arabia and sit there for three days

Graff has always believed that features one really big client; These days, a new generation Asia are coming through his

at any one time his list of clients
and as one door closes another one opens.
of clients from America, Europe and
open doors.

that would turn into three months, whilst Graff was entertaining clients daily in his shop. The only exception he made during these years of plenty was to go and visit the royal family of Brunei. He had a special relationship with them. He attended polo games with them; he was lent an Aston Martin to drive himself around the kingdom; he was royally entertained. At one stage he was going there virtually once a month and was a constant guest at the palace.

The Brunei patronage was, indeed, fabulous. It enabled Graff to express himself in what he designed and made.

It also enabled him to be financially liquid, and thus very strong in the diamond market at a time when the rest of the industry was depressed. This royal patronage meant he could buy very rare stones when they became available – the blues, the pinks, the yellows, the 'D' Flawless whites – and put magnificent and fabulous jewels together very fast. He was making everything from tiaras to necklaces to bracelets, expressing any and every idea possible in diamonds and gemstones.

The Middle Eastern families he had met on his travels were his first great group of supporters, followed by the Royal Family of Brunei, who were spending more and more time in London. Graff has always believed that at any one time his list of clients features one really big client; and as one door

Right: His Majesty the Sultan and the Queen of Brunei, an early and very important client of Graff. Corbis.

THE FABULOUS

closes another one opens. These days, a new generation of clients from America, Europe and Asia are coming through his open doors.

In the 1990s the influx of oil money began to tail off. The Brunei Royal Family visited London only twice a year, and the Arabs stayed at home. So he began to travel again – and he noticed that the world was changing and he wanted to reflect the changes he had observed with more refinement and style. He felt that the shop in Knightsbridge was dated in comparison with the beautiful shops on grand streets he had seen on his travels.

So he managed to secure a 19th-century townhouse in historic New Bond Street, at the time a quiet backwater and not the high-fashion centre it has now become.

In 1993 Graff was the first to restore an entire townhouse in the area to its former glory. It was officially opened by HRH Princess Michael of Kent. At the opening party Dame Shirley Bassey thrilled the guests by giving an impromptu concert in the shop. The large windows glittered with rare and beautiful stones, shown on rotating window displays, a system invented by Graff to enable jewels to be displayed from the front rather than the back as had been the custom.

At first this belle époque building was leasehold, but eventually its freehold became available together with five other properties on New Bond Street, and Graff

Graff owns substantial real estate surrounding his own store in New Bond Street, including the buildings illustrated, which are rented to other jewellers. His London headquarters are in two 18th century buildings in Albemarle Street.

bought them all. Subsequently, he has added more properties as they have come up and is now landlord to many other global luxury labels in Mayfair.

The success of the New Bond Street outlet in attracting international royalty, celebrities and the very rich started Graff thinking about opening similar retail shops abroad. A *salon privé* opened in Monte Carlo, on the mezzanine of the Hotel de Paris, which was a great success. Another shop was opened in Courchevel and then one in Geneva, together with regular exhibitions in the arcade shop at the Palace Hotel in St Moritz during the season – all of which are for clients going to Switzerland to ski.

Graff also realised that the U.S.A. was under-developed in terms of high-level retail jewellery shops. In 2001 he opened a shop on Madison Avenue. To celebrate this in typical Graff style, an exceptional and unique 'D' Flawless diamond of 100.57 carats, the Star of America, was unveiled to great acclaim at a star-studded opening that made Manhattan sit up and take notice.

The Madison Avenue store was followed by the purchase of a palatial 12,000 square foot U.S.A. corporate headquarters on 61st Street. There are now Graff stores in New York, Palm Beach, Las Vegas, Chicago and Bal Harbour. There is also an increasing number of concessions in Saks stores across America as well as the main shop in Saks Fifth Avenue.

Graff believes that the early years of finding clients, by travelling with 72

At the opening of the Graff New York store, which introduced the Star of America diamond.
1. George Hamilton and Princess Michael of Kent.
2. Mrs Laurence Graff, François Graff and Angelica Houston.
3. Count Roffredo, Ivana Trump, Mr and Mrs Laurence Graff.
4. The Star of America, an exceptional diamond of 100.57 carats.

sample rings to up-country Malaya or the Middle East, have gone forever. His major clients travel globally as a matter of course, and now almost anywhere they go they are never far from a Graff shop. Here they can be sure that the most fabulous jewellery in the world is in stock and for sale, and that they will always be able to find the perfect multi-coloured diamond *sautoir*, or a ring set with an historic diamond that could have belonged to a maharajah, or a glittering flash of Graff-cut gems.

For his growing number of clients in Asia there is a magnificent shop in Hong Kong, and the Graff empire has stretched ever outward to Tokyo and, in the Chinese century, to Shanghai and Beijing. Russia has always been a particular enthusiasm of his and this enthusiasm has been keenly reciprocated. Coming from a Russian and Eastern European background as he does, he had always wanted to go there. So, as soon as Perestroika was declared, he paid a visit that resulted in the first Graff store being opened in Moscow, followed by another outside the capital in the Luxury village, together with four other outlets. Then there are the sores in the Middle East, two in Wafi City, Dubai, and in Bahrain and Kuwait.

But Graff's expansion has not been limited to retail shops.

His business became the first in the international, and very competitive, diamond industry to be vertically integrated: able to take a diamond all the way from acquiring it in the rough through to selling it in one of his shops. Granted, Graff was already a dealer

Left: A diamond in the rough.

THE FABLE

in diamonds – the word 'retailer' did not sum Graff up at all. He had always been a diamond dealer, tendering for rough diamonds in Africa, Canada, Australia, Brazil, wherever diamonds are mined, and then transforming them into their purest state and presenting them to the public in the form of fabulous jewels. At about the same time Graff was offered the Hope of Africa diamond, the first big stone cut in Africa by Krochmal & Cohen from Johannesburg. One of the two partners, Johnny Kneller, was well known to Graff, who had bought diamonds from him and his father before him. When the Hope came in, he bought it in five minutes as it was so very rare, a 115.91-carat yellow diamond – so named to celebrate the release of Nelson Mandela from 28 years of captivity, and thus symbolising a new era of hope in the history of South Africa.

Krochmal & Cohen specialised in superior stones and fancy yellows, so Graff, having bought the Hope of Africa diamond, thought it a good idea to suggest that a bigger company be formed in order to obtain larger quantities of rough diamonds. He went out to buy a diamond and acquired a company, which they called the South African Diamond Corporation, or SAFDICO.

SAFDICO now has cutting operations in Antwerp and in Mauritius, where it has a majority shareholding in the Floreal Diamond Cutting factory. The factory in the U.S. focuses on important stones and, because it is located close to the Gemological Institute of America, handles the all-important certification of

Right: Main picture: Francois & Laurence Graff oversee the mining of diamonds from the rough to the finished design

Top left: Mrs Graff at a celebrity party.

Above left: Laurence Graff with their Royal Highnesses Prince and Princess Michael of Kent, on the occasion of the opening of the first Graff shop in Moscow.

Above: Emma Thompson wears Graff jewels for the Oscars.

Left: With Joan Collins at the opening of the New Bond Street townhouse store.

THE FABLE

Antwerp, on the other hand, is the selling arm for SAFDICO's diamonds, cutting parcels of rough stone that are sold on to an international trade clientele. SAFDICO has grown and flourished and it is now expanding further through the creation of a diamond park in Botswana. A 'Rhodes in reverse' operation (after Cecil Rhodes who started diamond production in South Africa in the 19th century) imports diamond sights to Botswana for cutting and polishing. The infrastructure of a huge park complex supports both SAFDICO and other major manufacturers bringing business to the country's stable government and economy.

In the 21st century the production of the most fabulous jewels in the world for all the many Graff stores is done mostly in Graff's headquarters, now in two adjacent 18th-century townhouses in Mayfair, restored to the splendour of their heyday as aristocrats' city palaces. From there a never-ending, glittering stream of gems flows out daily to Graff shops all over the world to be sold to the wealthiest clients on the planet.

Graff's long-time clients, cultivated on his pioneering voyages of the day before yesterday, have been joined by the sons, daughters and friends of the original clients Graff first met on his solitary journeys a lifetime ago.

Presidents, kings and queens, oligarchs, sheikhs and their sheikhas, hedge-fund billionaires, global celebrities, new-money billionaires from Russia, China or Japan are all familiar sights in Graff's elegant salons, drawn to the unique array of rare and precious stones set in the inimitable, fluid, slightly mysterious Graff style that aims to show the splendour of the component diamonds and gems in the design and flatter the wearer through settings that shimmer and move with the body.

Laurence Graff himself still symbolises the global brand he has built. His is a family business and he works with his son François, his brother Raymond and his nephew Elliot, but Graff still oversees the finding and production of the unique, large and rare gems he has always loved with a passion. He is passing on to those close to him the minutiae of the jewellers' trade, which has been his lifetime's vocation and which in its global, 21st-century incarnation owes much to his sense of adventure and innovation.

The story of how a one-man business in a tiny workshop in Hatton Garden has grown into a global brand is a contemporary fable. The name Graff is known all over the world of wealth and fame as it always delivers the most fabulous jewels in the world.

The poor East End boy has truly become the King of Diamonds.

Laurence Graff with Andy Warhol's *Lilac Marilyn*.

Graff has owned some of the most beautiful and rarest diamonds in the world; rare because of their size, colour or quality, or rare because of their history. His advertising always confidently says that he sells 'the most fabulous jewels in the world'. And he does. Whether it is a pair of huge canary yellow diamonds that were given by Edward VIII to Wallis Simpson, later Duchess of Windsor, a diamond like a ray of sunlight that belonged to a long-dead maharajah, or a diamond that belonged to a tragic emperor, Graff uses only the very best stones, both historic and modern, to make extraordinary pieces of jewellery.

There has got to be mystique in a jewel, something mysterious and beautiful about it to capture the imagination.

He believes that, bearing this in mind, Graff jewels are never really in fashion so they don't go out of fashion, they have a mysterious identity all of their own. 'We don't follow trends, we do what we do,' he says. So what makes a Graff piece a Graff piece? To Graff himself it's very simple. 'Right from the beginning, it has always been the stones. When you have the very best stones then you can really work away to produce a marvellous piece of jewellery.'

When Graff sees an extraordinary stone for the first time he knows he is going to buy it: 'I don't hesitate, I just buy it, but, as a trader, it is a great responsibility buying a

Laurence Graff with *Red Liz* by Andy Warhol.
Right: Jane Seymour wears a Graff ruby and diamond necklace.

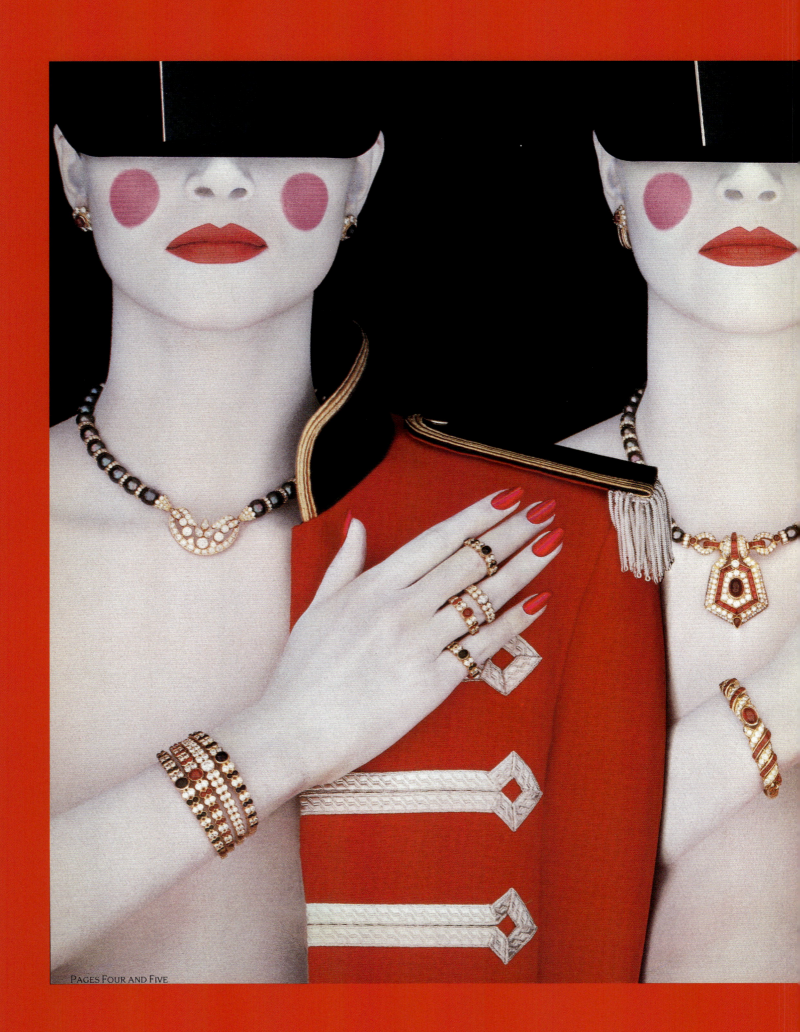

Pages Four and Five

very rare stone. You go by instinct and it takes a lot of judgment and investment. But when you buy such a stone, you are not just a trader, you are a collector and custodian of the stone while you own it. When I buy such an extraordinary stone, I always know I have done the right thing, because of what the stone is. It is unique. And,' he points out,

'A diamond can never be too big. I have never seen a diamond that couldn't be worn. They are never, ever vulgar.'

Graff's jewels are deceptively simple in design terms. As he explains, 'The Graff "look" depends on how you knit the stones together, how you play with them, how you lay them out.' None of his early designs was done with a pen or paintbrush, which is the way most jewellery is designed, but by Graff himself 'sitting at a table with the stones, sorting them into ranges, laying them out in shapes. I then take wax and make a three-dimensional model'.

He worked in this manner because his early pieces, starting with the original ring of 33 diamonds, used a great many small stones to create a 'big flash'. 'I used the stones to make a shape and then filled that shape up with small diamonds. I didn't make *pavé* pieces until midway through my career when there was a boom in slightly less expensive pieces which couldn't take too many big stones, so I started using *pavé* settings in flower shapes and animalistic forms.'

Graff always talks of his designs as being like knitting with jewellery because 'it's so soft, so subtle after you have put the stones together and joined them up'. He likes his jewels to be very mobile so that

When a woman wears a piece it becomes sensual when she moves – 'you can see the stones shimmer and move too'.

He invented the wire setting in which there is a collet, a little gap of wire, then another collet. The collet takes the stone, then there is a little peg, another collet and a peg, another collet and a space. 'You can open it up and you then get free-form waterfalls and tassels. Everybody has copied this setting, but it is a natural evolution of previous ways of setting, notably in the 18th century.'

In the mid-1980s coloured diamonds became extremely desirable. They had been out of favour for nearly two centuries, but people in Hong Kong, Singapore and Brunei started buying them. Graff became enthralled by these rare diamonds, which were (and are) few and far between. 'Then, as luck would have it, the Australians discovered the Argyle mine, which yielded up a small amount of pink diamonds. I tendered on the first pinks and bought all of them for $3.5 million. It was unheard of,' he remembers. 'Other professionals thought I was too adventurous; they didn't believe they would sell. They were really small stones, mostly 0.25 of a carat to one carat, of an unusual

'I look at historic European jewellery past and present. I am inspired by tribal jewellery, the exquisite craft and by shapes, forms, patterns and different things I see around me but I also look at costume jewellery Moghul jewels from India, African of traditional Asian jewellery prints, flowers and animals. So many inspire me '

Left: Portrait of Lady Jane Grey by Holbein: Bridgeman.

Above: Graff made this Renaissance-inspired diamond and carved emerald pendant using an emerald which had belonged to Princess Margaret.

pink colour that hadn't been seen before.' As with his original 33-diamond ring, Graff decided to use all the pinks to make one single big creation and produced a magnificent *tremblant* flower.

Tremblant flowers are not new, they date back to the 18th century and had a revival in the 1930s. Graff's contemporary version was composed of all the different sizes and shapes of pink diamonds from the Argyle mine put together in one fabulous piece. 'It was amazing!' he says. 'I remember it was finished at four o'clock one afternoon and just then I had a call from the Sultan of Brunei who granted me an audience at the Dorchester – he had just bought the hotel. During our meeting, he asked me if I had anything I would like to show him. I had slipped this amazing piece into my pocket and while we were talking I pulled out the flower and said "Your Majesty, what do you think of this?" He opened his hands to have a look at it and I could see his eyes gleam with excitement at this absolutely unique and beautiful jewel and I sold it to him in two minutes. I was out of all the pink diamonds in two minutes!'

It wasn't easy to acquire 'D' Flawless white diamonds or the blues, yellows and the pinks. But Graff, in a time of innovation, reacted to the adventurous mood of the era and started to create multi-coloured diamond jewellery. 'The newness of the radiant cut inspired me to create pieces that had never been created before,' he says. Other jewellers tried to copy him, but Graff had already become synonymous with these rare designs in coloured diamonds.

Madame de Pompadour by François Boucher: Bridgeman.

Dilip Singh,
Maharajah of Lahore
1854,
painted by
Franz Xavier Winterhalter:
Bridgeman.

Photograph of Queen Alexandra by Walery: National Portrait Gallery.

Left: A Maasai bride in Kenya.

Greta Garbo in *Mata Hari:* Corbis.

André Marty, *La Gazette de Bon Ton*, 1922.

As Graff bought more and more stones, he had to find more and more ways to set them. 'I made incredible creations surrounded by pink diamonds, yellow diamonds, blue diamonds and they became more and more valuable.'

Before any really important diamond is incorporated into a necklace, a ring or a bracelet at Graff, it is given a name if it doesn't have one and sometimes a book about it is put together to give to the eventual owner. These books tell the story of the stone as it emerges from the rough in the cutting. Photographs are taken as the diamond progresses from its rough state to its final brilliance. Then Graff will create a beautiful jewel using the stone as a centrepiece in an intricate and glittering spider's web.

But Graff doesn't just design jewels around the centrepiece of a large and rare or historic diamond. The house also sells 'designed' jewellery too, such as the waterfall jewellery where a myriad stones flow down in a shimmering, fluid mass. It makes necklaces and other pieces, weaving together diamonds and coloured gems – rubies, emeralds and sapphires. 'When we have an exhibition, coloured stones add to the excitement, to the spectrum of all the gems,' Graff contends. 'What we do is design,' he points out, 'but it is always very simple, very classical to show off the diamonds.'

But where does he get his ideas, of which there seem to be a never-ending stream? Had he ever been inspired by historic jewels? 'I am inspired by everything,' Graff responds. 'I look at historic European jewellery, but I also look at costume jewellery

past and present. I am inspired by Moghul jewels from India, African tribal jewellery and traditional Asian jewellery. Shapes, forms, flowers, animals and trees inspire me. And I look at what people are wearing.' He has always studied books on design, on wallpaper design, on carpets, on Western, Islamic and Indian art.

The long voyages he made in his youth opened his mind to other cultures and art, and gave him many ideas based upon those travels. He continues to travel for inspiration; to Morocco, for instance, to look at the palaces and see the shapes and patterns of carpets and tiles. The Russian crown jewels in the Hermitage have inspired him. He noted a cross in one of the crowns and, when diamond crosses became very desirable, he created one cross inspired by his glimpse of the crown of Monomakh. His many visits to Africa gave him ideas based on tribal jewellery and his travels in the Far East also opened his mind to the jewels of Asia.

He also visits museum shows such as an exhibition of Holbein court portraits. 'In his portraits, all the men and women were wearing rings,' he says. 'I have never seen rings that have better shapes than those rings, and I knew they would inspire future designs. I am always looking for new ideas to work on.' A passionate collector of modern and contemporary art, Graff does not cite one particular artist as a special inspiration for his designs, but rather says that his influences are widespread. 'I can't say I am influenced by all design. One looks back and one gets feelings that spark off a train of thought. But because the gems that I deal with today are so valuable and so

beautiful,' he points out, 'I find that most people want to see the gem, so most settings are very simple, they are just knitted together.

'It is interesting though how our wire settings are inspired by the past. The Moghul jewellers in India created masterpieces using the extraordinary stones which belonged to the maharajahs, jewels which started to get bigger and bigger. I have,' says Graff, 'always been fascinated by such antique jewels. I find them genuinely inspiring and have brought these looks forward and modernised them. You might say that I am influenced by every piece of jewellery that was ever created. But in spite of all these influences, I still produce jewels that are simple yet have that subtle mystique that I think all great jewels should have.'

Right: Laurence Graff with Pablo Picasso's *Aubade*.

Laurence Graff in his London boardroom,
with 'Untitled Chinese Painting' by Julian Schnabel.
Photograph: Andrey Bronnikov

THE
JEW

THE SULTAN'S DIAMONDS

The Idol's Eye

Abdul Hamid II, the 34th Ottoman Sultan, formed a huge collection of jewels that adorned his many wives and concubines in the harem at the Topkapi Palace. One of his most prized possessions was the Idol's Eye: a diamond of 70.21 carats, in shape something between an old mine cut and a triangular brilliant, with a very slight bluish tinge. This had been mined in the Golconda mines in Hyderabad in about 1600. Its first owner was, by repute, the Persian Prince Rahab, from whom it was sequestrated by the East India Company against a debt. Another myth is that it was the eye of an idol in Benghazi, hence its name, but this is unlikely as Benghazi has been Muslim since the 8th century.

What is certain about the stone is that it appeared at auction on 4 July 1865 described as 'a large, splendid diamond known as the Idol's Eye, set round with 18 smaller brilliants and a frame of small brilliants'. It was sold to a buyer known as B.B. who might have represented the Ottoman Sultan, already known as a prolific collector of unique and precious jewels. The Sultan was deposed in 1909, but not before he had sent his jewels to safety. The stone ended up in Paris, the property of the dealer Salomon Habib, who sold it to a Spanish grandee. It remained in a safety deposit box in London until the end of World War II, when it was sold to a New York dealer, who then sold it to May Bonfils Stanton of Colorado. The heiress of a newspaper fortune, Mrs Stanton was typical of those obsessed with diamonds and had collected important stones since she was a girl.

Right: The Idol's Eye diamond: 70.21 carats.

She lived in an isolated mansion reputedly copied from the Petit Trianon at Versailles. She was rumoured to wear the Idol's Eye every morning at her solitary breakfast. After her death in 1962 it came up for auction at Sotheby's and, over a decade later, came into the possession of Laurence Graff. It was the first historic diamond he bought.

'I looked into the stone,' he remembers. 'It was more interesting than beautiful. But when I learnt about its history, I got very taken by it. It was a light blue, but not a fancy blue, and when I first saw it, I intended to cut it into a heart shape because it was already similar in shape. Then I thought, "with all this history, I shouldn't touch it", so I decided to reset it in the original diamond necklace that I had bought it in.'

The Sultan Abdul Hamid II Diamond

Weighing 70.54 carats this is an antique brilliant cut fancy light yellow diamond also owned by the Sultan which, when it was bought by Graff in 1981, was set as a brooch with diamond sprays. Graff reset it as the focal stone for a superb necklace with a fringe effect falling from the diamond.

Left: The Sultan Abdul Hamid II Diamond: 70.54 carats.

THE JEWELS

Above: The Idol's Eye (70.21 carats), suspended from its original necklace.
Inset: May Bonfils Stanton.

THE JEWELS

At the Graff launch of the Idol's Eye.

DIAMOND IMPERIAL

The Emperor Maximilian Diamond

This is one of two diamonds named after the tragic Archduke Maximilian of Austria (1832-1867), Emperor of Mexico, supposedly bought by him in Brazil in 1850 during his first visit to the New World on a botanical expedition. It is 41.94 carats, a cushion antique cut modified brilliant.

In 1863, under pressure from Napoleon III, Maximilian consented to accept the Mexican crown, and landed at Vera Cruz on 28 May 1864. From the outset his reign was troubled and by 1866 it was obvious that he should abdicate. However, Maximilian refused to desert his followers. His wife, the Empress Carlotta, returned to Europe to plead for help. But in 1867 Maximilian was court-martialled, sentenced to death and executed by firing squad. This story captured the imagination of Manet, who depicted the scene in his work *The Execution of Maximilian*, a fragment of which is in the National Gallery.

Legend has it that the Emperor was wearing the Emperor Maximilian Diamond round his neck in a small bag when he faced the firing squad. Following the execution, his remains were returned to Europe and the diamond to his widow. Subsequently it was sold to help pay expenses during her mental illness. It then disappeared for nearly half a century until 1919 when it was purchased by a Chicago gem dealer and subsequently displayed at the 1934 Chicago World's Fair. Mr Hotz always refused to sell the diamond and it remained in his possession until his death. Subsequently, it was acquired by a titled private owner who sent it for sale in 1982.

Left: The Emperor Maximilian Diamond: 41.94 carats.

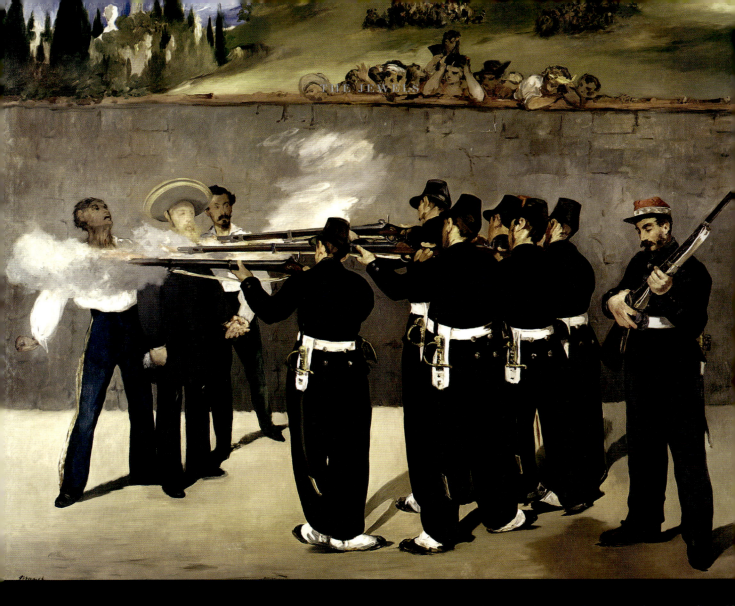

'The Emperor Maximilian Diamond was not a high-coloured stone,' says Graff 'but it was fascinating. It had fascinating fluorescence and I just had to have it. I overpaid for it, because of its history.' At the time Graff used an advertising agency who came up with the idea of dressing a woman in a Maximilian costume similar to a portrait of the Emperor. 'We went to a tailor who made a costume – the first one was blue,' Graff remembers, 'and the idea was to photograph a model, but not her whole face, just her lips, the costume and the piece of jewellery.'

The resulting advertisement was so radically different from any other jewellery advertisements of the time that it caused a lot of attention. 'Over the years, we changed the colour of the uniform,' Graff says. 'White, red, green, and we wove the word "Graff" into its material.'

Above: The Execution of Maximilian 1870 by Manet: Bridgeman.
Right: Graff advertising inspired by Imperial uniforms.

THE JEWELS

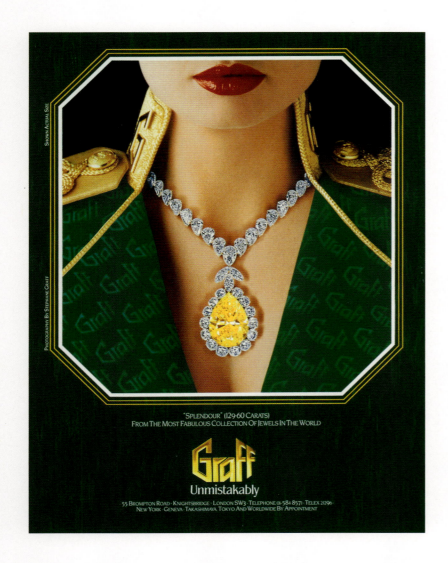

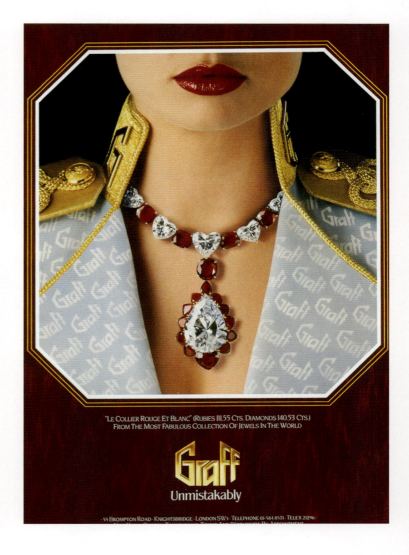

108

THE JEWELS

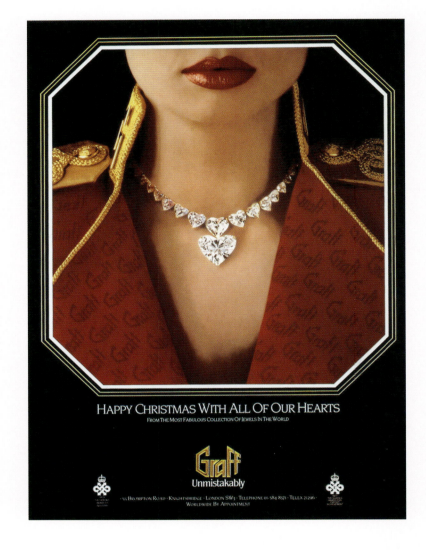

THE PHILIPPINES EPISODE

In the early 1980s, Graff was invited to visit the Philippines after a lady-in-waiting to Madame Marcos, wife of the President, saw an exhibition he had put on in Hong Kong. He went to Manila with three stones – the Idol's Eye, the Sultan Abdul Hamid II Diamond and the Emperor Maximilian Diamond – and was invited to the Malacanang Palace for an audience with Madame Marcos. That evening Graff was invited on the presidential yacht for dinner. He arrived with the three diamonds in his pocket and, an hour later, the President and Madame Marcos arrived on board. 'The yacht pulled away from the quay and started to cruise round the harbour – or so I thought. I was,' he remembers, 'having a great time. I suddenly wondered where we were going because I could see the lights in the harbour getting dimmer and dimmer and I realised we were going out to sea surrounded by warships.'

At five in the morning, the yacht slowed down and Graff thought it had come back into port, but it hadn't. 'We had arrived on Bamboo Island, a private island owned by the Marcoses, where everything was made from bamboo; the houses, the furniture, everything. I was given a house to myself and a wardrobe of *barong tagalongs* [traditional Filipino formal shirts]. I remember phoning home saying, "don't worry about me, I've been kidnapped by the President and his wife."' They stayed on Bamboo Island for nearly a week, during which Graff sold the three diamonds for a figure in excess of $10 million. 'It was the biggest diamond deal ever to one individual at the time – although,' says Graff, 'much larger transactions have happened since.'

Right: Madame Imelda Marcos photographed by Norman Parkinson: Corbis.

THE JEWELS

THE JEWELS

A DIAMOND FOR THE QUEEN OF ROMANCE

The Deepdene Diamond

The Deepdene Diamond was thought to have been discovered in 1890 in South Africa and was named Deepdene after the estate of its first owner, Cary Bok, who eventually loaned it to the Academy of Natural Science in Philadelphia. In about 1954, the stone was sold to an anonymous American buyer. Thirty years later it was put up for auction in Geneva by the German jeweller who then owned it and it was purchased by a French jeweller – rumour had it that it was on behalf of Aristotle Onassis.

'The Deepdene was a troubled stone,' says Graff. 'It was sold as an untreated stone to the French jewellers and they had a problem with it. When they tested it, it was thought to have been irradiated. In the end, the stone came back on the market but there were still questions as to whether it had been irradiated or not. I bought it for about $700,000 – a great buy. It is 104.52 carats, cushion cut of a wonderful fancy golden-yellow colour. It was an amazing diamond and we studied it and decided not to repolish it, which I had thought of doing, but to leave it. Later, I sold the diamond to Danielle Steele, one of the most successful novelists in the world today. It is one of her favourite diamonds.'

Above: Danielle Steele: Getty Images
Right: The Deepdene Diamond: 104.52 carats.

THE MARLBOROUGH DIAMOND MYSTERY

The Marlborough Diamond

On 11 September 1980, Laurence Graff was quietly sitting in his office at the back of his Knightsbridge shop reading a telegram, when he saw two masked men burst into the shop and heard them tell his staff and clients to lie face down on the floor. Graff stayed where he was, hidden from sight, while one of the men cleared out the window display and the other picked out a necklace which contained a magnificent 45.47-carat antique brilliant cushion cut white stone called The Marlborough Diamond. 'It wasn't the finest white diamond I had ever seen,' Graff comments, 'but its previous history had attracted me to it.'

It was so called because it had belonged to Gladys Deacon, a famous American beauty and intellectual, the second wife of the 9th Duke of Marlborough. In her youth she had dazzled society in Paris, Rome and London. In 1902, she was so well-known that cardboard dolls named 'Miss Deacon' were on sale to the general public. Proust had admired her, so had Anatole France. Epstein had sculpted her, Boldini had painted and drawn her. But her marriage to the Duke was not happy and she ended her days as a veiled recluse as a result of a failed operation on her face.

The police had a single clue as to the perpetrators. Their getaway car's number had been taken by a passerby. It was easily traced and so were the thieves – they had rented the car using their own identities.

After abandoning their car, the thieves took a taxi and stopped at a post office where the driver was asked to post a parcel. From there they went to Heathrow Airport and

Right: The Marlborough Diamond: 45.47 carats.

home to Chicago. Here, Joseph Scalise, known as 'Witherhand' because he had been born minus four fingers on his left hand, and Arthur 'The Genius' Rachel, a thief and counterfeiter known for his brilliance, were arrested at the airport and their bags searched, but no diamond was found.

Both men stood trial, were convicted in the U.K. and served thirteen years apiece at Parkhurst Prison on the Isle of Wight. Much later, interviewed on television, Scalise admitted he had taken the diamond but didn't know where it was. The trail was cold and The Marlborough Diamond has never been found. Maybe it was stolen to order and ended up in a private collection. But Laurence Graff may have the last laugh. 'The Idol's Eye, which I had bought a year or two before, was also in the shop that day,' he says. 'It was worth far, far more than the Marlborough and I suspect it was this diamond they were really after. But they missed it.'

Right: Gladys, Duchess of Marlborough: National Portrait Gallery.

Gladys, Duchess of Marlborough
Mark Gertler's back

THE BRUNEI ADVENTURE

Magnificent jewels for a royal family: Le Grand Coeur d'Afrique Diamond and Le Petit Coeur d'Afrique Diamond

When Brunei celebrated Independence in 1985, Mr and Mrs Laurence Graff and their son François attended the celebration as guests of the Royal Family. This was the culmination of an increasingly friendly relationship with His Majesty Sultan Haji Hassanal Bolkiah Mu'izzadin Waddaulah, the 29th Sultan of Brunei Darussalam, and his wife, Her Majesty The Raja Isteri Pengiran Anak Saleha.

On his voyages around East Asia, Graff had met the then Crown Prince and his wife during their frequent visits to Singapore and often visited Brunei, where he began to sell jewels to the Sultan and other members of the Royal Family. The jewels became more and more elaborate. 'The ladies used to wear long dresses on which were pinned three brooches of semi-precious stones joined up on a chain. I started to do versions set with diamonds, and connected with a diamond chain, which met with their approval.'

Graff became more daring, buying more and more stones to make the elaborate pieces. 'I made incredible creations surrounded by pink, blue and yellow diamonds, inspired by the Malay jewellery tradition and by motifs I had seen in Persian rugs. Often the major stones in these pieces would be unique, historic diamonds I had found, or very large modern ones I had had cut and polished. The pieces got bigger and bigger and became more and more valuable because we were selling more and more stones set into one piece of jewellery.'

Right: Le Grande Coeur d'Afrique Diamond (70.03 carats) and Le Petit Coeur d'Afrique Diamond (25.22 carats) set in a heart-shaped diamond necklace.

THE JEWELS

Over the years, the Sultan has bought many extraordinary diamonds from Graff. In 1982, for instance, he bought Le Grand Coeur d'Afrique Diamond, a 70.03-carat stone, the largest heart-shaped diamond in the world, which has a sibling, Le Petit Coeur d'Afrique Diamond, a 25.22-carat diamond, also heart-shaped. 'The diamonds came from Conakry, the capital of Guinea, and they were fabulous! Fabulous!' exclaims Graff. He set them both into a necklace in which Le Grand Coeur suspends from Le Petit Coeur. 'I sold it to the Sultan and it was the first really major piece he bought from me.' There were many, many more.

HISTORIC INDIAN DIAMONDS

The Star of Bombay Diamond, the Maharajah Diamond and the Golconda 'D' Diamond.

Since the time of the Moghul emperors the Golconda mines in the Kingdom of Golconda, now part of the Indian state of Hyderabad, have produced some of the most historic and beautiful diamonds, notable for their soft brilliance. Graff has owned many of these unique stones. The Star of Bombay Diamond, an unnamed yellow diamond of 47.39 carats, was the first major diamond that was named by Laurence Graff. He bought it in 1974 from a European dealer, who sold it for the benefit of a noble Indian family. 'It was emerald cut and it had probably been set in a maharajah's regalia,' Graff believes. The Maharajah Diamond is, as Graff describes it, 'my diamond at any price'. An old mine brilliant cut diamond of 78.10 carats, it was in a bank for 50 years before Graff bought it in 2006. He sold it the next day. 'I owned, even for 24 hours, one of the most beautiful diamonds in the world, because of its clear brilliance like a star. The translucency, the life in that stone, is beyond anything I have ever seen.'

The Golconda 'D' Diamond was a 'D' Flawless 47.29-carat antique brilliant cut stone. 'It was a round diamond, and very, very rare because it is unusual to find such quality in large stones,' says Graff. 'It had come from an Indian family and ended up in New York, where I bought it in 1984 from a dealer selling it on behalf of an aristocratic family. I made it into a single stone ring, which I sold to a Middle Eastern family for $5 million. It was the largest 'D' Flawless brilliant cut diamond in the world. Years later, I cut the Icon Diamond, another 'D' Flawless brilliant round diamond which was double the size.'

Right: The Star of Bombay Diamond: 47.39 carats.

Above: The Golconda 'D' Diamond: 47.29 carats.
Right: The Maharajah Diamond: 78.10 carats.

BLUE AND ROSE

The Imperial Blue Diamond and The Empress Rose Diamond

The Imperial Blue Diamond is a 39.31-carat flawless pear-shaped diamond and, at the time Graff acquired it in 1984, it was the largest blue diamond in the world. At the same time, Graff possessed the largest pink diamond, The Empress Rose Diamond, at 72.79 carats, also pear-shaped. 'Can you imagine! I owned the largest blue diamond in the world at the same time as the largest pink diamond. I remember doing the double-page advertisements for these two extraordinary diamonds, using the Graff uniform; one page was blue and the other side was pink.' Perhaps this advertisement, more than any other, signified that Graff had become a force to be reckoned with in the rarefied world of important and rare diamonds because, as he explains, 'I had stones of a size and colour few people had ever seen before.'

Right: The Imperial Blue Diamond: 39.31 carats.

The Empress Rose Diamond: 72.79 carats.

EXCELSIOR

The Excelsior I Diamond

In 1893 a worker at the Jagersfontein mine in South Africa found the largest rough diamond in the world at the time, when he saw it in the gravel he was shovelling into his truck. Weighing an astonishing 995.2 carats, it was only superseded by the Cullinan Diamond, found twelve years later and now part of the British Crown Jewels. The Excelsior still remains the second largest rough diamond ever mined. The worker who found it hid this astonishing rough diamond from his overseer and delivered it directly to the mine manager, who rewarded him with a horse, a saddle and bridle, and the enormous sum of £500 in cash.

The name Excelsior – meaning higher – was inspired by the original shape of the stone, which was flat on one side and rose to a peak on the other. It was of a pure blue white in colour. It wasn't cut until ten years after it had been found, when it was entrusted to Asscher's Diamond Co. in Amsterdam, the leading diamond cutters of the day. Asscher decided to cut the stone into several smaller diamonds, rather than one large stone, as there were quite a number of black spots within the original rough diamond. So it was cut into 21 diamonds, the largest being 69.68 carats and known as the Excelsior I; and it is this magnificent diamond that Graff bought in 1984. Subsequently, he sold it to a member of the Saudi Arabian Royal Family for over $7 million.

Right: The Excelsior I Diamond: 69.68 carats.

THE WINDSOR YELLOWS

The Windsor Yellow Diamonds

In 1987 the most successful jewellery auction ever was held in Geneva of the jewels belonging to Wallis Simpson, Duchess of Windsor, one of the most fashionable and famous women in the world. The potent combination of the greatest love story of the 20th century, which led to the abdication and exile of the King of England, and the quality and design of the jewels the Duke of Windsor had made for his Duchess, became an international sensation.

Laurence Graff was amongst the major bidders at this sale, televised all over the world, and acquired two of the most famous and top lots. The Duchess was often photographed in the Windsor Yellows, a pair of clips of fancy yellow pear-shaped diamonds of 51.01 and 40.22 carats respectively, which Graff bought. 'I also bought another pair of clips the Duchess had owned,' he explains. 'Of course they needed re-cutting to bring them to their full potential. I bought all four, re-polished them, and eventually made the Windsor earrings, which were then bought by Rafic Hariri, then Prime Minister and founder of the new Lebanon, of which he was the single driving force in rebuilding. He bought the Windsor earrings to celebrate his re-election as Prime Minister, and as a gift for his wife.'

Graff also bought the most historic and sentimental piece of all: the Duchess of Windsor's 19-carat emerald engagement ring. 'It is one of the finest emeralds I have ever seen,' he says. 'The story is that the Duke, whilst still King, wanted to give Wallis Simpson, as she then was, a major emerald for an engagement ring. An equerry was

The Windsor Yellows. *Above*: When Graff acquired them at auction.
Below: After Graff had re-polished and reset them.

asked to inquire whether any such stones were available and a merchant in India was employed to search amongst the treasuries of historic stones owned by the princely families for the most fabulous emerald he could find. 'Originally, this stone was a bead – a *briolette* – which was subsequently cut in half to become two emeralds. This half was the superior gem, the other half was of much lower quality,' Graff explains. 'I've got the original jeweller's invoice, which was made out to "The King."' Graff gave the ring to his wife, Anne-Marie, for their 25th wedding anniversary.

Above: Mr and Mrs Rafic Hariri: Corbis.

A QUEEN, AN EMPRESS, A DUCHESS, A MAHARANI

The Porter Rhodes Diamond

The Porter Rhodes Diamond is generally believed to be one of the finest ever found in South Africa. It was mined during the very early days of the Kimberley mine, discovered in February 1880. It is a colourless octahedron weighing 54.04 carats and it originally belonged to Porter Rhodes, one of the first directors of the South African diamond mines. So rare and beautiful did he think it that Porter Rhodes sent his extraordinary pure white stone to London, where a reputable dealer and gemmologist of the time, Edwin Streeter, exhibited it at his office.

Word reached Queen Victoria of the existence of this extraordinary diamond, through her Crown Jeweller at the time, and Rhodes was asked to travel to the Queen's residence, Osborne House on the Isle of Wight, to show her the stone. Queen Victoria was extremely knowledgeable about diamonds, possessing as she did many rare and beautiful examples, including the Koh I Noor, part of the Crown Jewels, and she wondered whether the stone had really come from the Cape, hitherto considered as a source of lesser diamonds.

Next, the deposed Empress Eugenie of France, living in a cottage on the Queen's estate, also asked to see the stone. She was also an expert on diamonds, having had the use, while still Empress of France, of the royal cabinet of jewels, which included many historic diamonds collected by Louis XIV, Louis XV and Louis XVI. She too thought it was so beautiful and pure a white that it could not have come from the Cape, it having been thought that Cape diamonds were usually yellowish in colour.

Right: The Porter Rhodes Diamond: 54.04 carats.

It could thus be said that the Porter Rhodes Diamond single-handedly established the reputation of diamonds from the Cape.

The pure white diamond was fashioned into an old-mine cut stone and eventually, in 1930, the Duke of Westminster bought it as a present for his third wife, Loelia. Following their divorce, it passed to a jeweller who had it re-cut into an emerald cut of 54.04 carats It was bought by that arbiter of taste and lover of rare jewels, the Maharajah of Indore. It then passed to owners in Philadelphia and Texas and was finally acquired by Graff in 1987 for $3,800,000. 'I decided no one would buy that diamond but me,' he recalls. 'Eventually, I sold it to the Royal Family of Brunei. It was a really beautiful, beautiful diamond.'

Above left: Queen Victoria: Corbis.
Above right: The Empress Eugenie: Corbis.
Right: The Duchess of Westminster: Sotheby's/Beaton Archive.

THE JEWELS

REDS

The Mogok Ruby and the Graff Ruby

'The Mogok Ruby was one of the finest ever seen by anybody,' says Graff. The Mogok Stone Tract in upper Burma has been worked since 1597, when the King of Burma secured the mines, but they became internationally famous for producing beautiful deep crimson pigeon's blood rubies when the British took them over in 1886. Since the communist regime came to power in Burma in 1963, the Mogok region has been off limits to foreigners but is still producing wonderful gems. 'When I saw it, the Mogok Ruby belonged to a New Yorker who had boasted for twenty years that he had the finest ruby in the world,' Laurence Graff recounts. 'But eventually he decided to donate the proceeds of its sale to charity, and I bought it in 1987 for a little over $3,500,000.' Until Graff acquired this ruby, he had never seen one to compare with it. Cushion cut, it weighs 15.97 carats. Later it was sold to a European client.

The Graff Ruby, a cushion cut Burmese ruby of 8.62 carats, was also from the Mogok mine and was set in a ring. 'Tavernier, who sought out rare stones for Louis XIV, once said, "Any ruby over 5 carats has no price." This stone has no price. This ruby,' Graff says, 'is the ruby of all rubies. I mounted it into a fabulous ring – a ruby of this calibre and weight is very, very rare and I had to pay a world-record price for it.'

Right: The Mogok Ruby: 15.97 carats.

Above: The Graff Ruby: 8.62 carats.

TIARAS

Tiaras, or 'fenders' as the Edwardians used to call them, may seem an anachronism in the 21st-century world, dating back to an earlier, grander age. Far from it. Still obligatory when an invitation reads, 'Decorations', they are worn for state dinners and balls in Britain, and the British Royal Family owns some superb historic examples. It is, however, rare to see them being worn at a private dance. But tiaras are still very much de rigueur in the Middle East and in South East Asia, where they are much in demand at very grand weddings, one of which might necessitate a different tiara for every day of the celebration.

Over the years, Graff has made extraordinary contemporary tiaras for queens, princesses and the wives of heads of state, including a tiara made entirely of pink diamonds for the Queen of Brunei. His tiaras have featured at royal Middle Eastern weddings, at grand society balls and in exhibitions of the jeweller's art. 'We always have tiaras in our shops for our clients and it is surprising how many we sell,' says Graff.

HEARTS

The Morning Star Diamond, the Star of Lesotho, the Birthday Diamond, the Golden Africa Diamond

Heart-shaped diamonds are one of the distinguishing marks of Graff jewels and he has owned and set some superb examples of romantic jewels over the years. The Morning Star is 46.44 carats and was set as a pendant in a necklace of diamond hearts. The Star of Lesotho, a 'D' coloured heart-shaped diamond of 53.11 carats, was acquired in 2005 and also set in a necklace of heart-shaped diamonds. The Birthday Diamond, a 'D' Flawless diamond of 56.42 carats, was so-called because the stone was finished on 13 June, Laurence Graff's birthday. Another notable heart-shaped diamond acquired and re-polished by Graff was the Golden Africa Diamond, a fancy intense yellow diamond of 50.80 carats.

Right: The Golden Africa Diamond: 50.80 carats.

Left: The Star of Lesotho: 53.11 carats.
Above: The Birthday Diamond: 56.42 carats.

The Morning Star Diamond: 46.44 carats.

ETERNAL LIGHT

La Favorite Diamond, the Eternal Light Diamond, the Excellence Diamond and the Icon Diamond

La Favorite Diamond was mined in South Africa and first made a public appearance at the Chicago World's Fair in 1933. At the time, it was owned by a Persian and valued at the enormous sum, for those days, of one million dollars. At the height of the Depression, this long emerald cut 'D' coloured diamond of 50.01 carats was a huge sensation and attracted enormous queues.

It was subsequently set in a ring and Graff acquired the diamond in New York in 2001 for $3,636,000. 'It was an amazing stone which I bought during the week in which we opened the New York store,' he remembers. 'It was also the same week we finished the Star of America Diamond. That was a major week for me! We kept the diamond for three or four years and then sold it, but I loved that diamond, it was a special stone with wonderful associations for me.'

The Eternal Light Diamond at 85.91 carats was one of the first of the large new stones to come up for auction in 1987. It was pear-shaped, 'D' Flawless and no one was selling such big stones at the time except Graff, who paid $10 million for it and kept it for just ten months before selling it to a member of a Royal Family.

The Excellence Diamond of 50.01 carats was a 'D' Flawless emerald cut stone which belonged to the singer and film star Pia Zadora, who was painted by Andy Warhol. Graff then sold the stone to a Parisienne, who sold it back to Graff some years later – he immediately made it into a magnificent ring.

Right: La Favorite Diamond: 50.01 carats.

The Icon Diamond, now called the Safia, is, as Graff puts it, 'a most unbelievable diamond' of 90.97 carats, 'D' Flawless and round – the largest round 'D' Flawless diamond in the world, cut from a piece of rough of over 300 carats which he had bought in South Africa direct from the mine. It took several days to negotiate the price. It was finished just in time for the opening of the Monte Carlo Salon and was the star of a gala evening at the Monte Carlo casino for 350 guests. 'Ironically, one invited guest who did not attend called to see the stone the next day, bought it for over $12.5 million and renamed it the Safia after his wife.'

Right: The Icon Diamond: 90.97 carats.

Above: The Excellence Diamond: 50.01 carats.
Right: The Eternal Light Diamond: 85.91 carats.

THE BLUES

The Begum Blue, the Graff Blue Heart, the Whitney Blue

The Begum Blue Diamond was the largest fancy deep blue heart-shaped diamond to have appeared at auction at the time and can be compared, as its cataloguing suggested, with some of the finest historical examples of blue diamonds ever, including the Idol's Eye and the Graff Blue Heart. The Begum Blue, weighing 13.78 carats, was set in a necklace by Poiray, and suspended from a heart-shaped diamond of 16.03 carats, which in turn was suspended from a line of heart-shaped diamonds. This magnificent necklace had belonged to Princess Salimah Begum Aga Khan, who sold most of her jewellery after her divorce. This attracted a great deal of attention at the time, focusing on this necklace and its magnificent heart-shaped blue diamond, the Begum Blue. Graff acquired it for over $7 million.

The magnificent Graff Blue Heart, at 6.68 carats, is a beautiful deep blue colour, flawless and cut as a perfect heart shape. It was purchased in New York and originally owned by a well-respected aristocratic European family who left Europe for the U.S. at the turn of the last century.

The Whitney Blue Diamond originally belonged to Betsey Cushing Roosevelt Whitney, one of three famously beautiful and elegant Cushing sisters, daughters of a fiercely ambitious upper-middle class Boston mother, who married them all off extremely well to American aristocracy– several times over.

Above: Princess Salimah Aga Khan.
Right: The Begum Blue Diamond: 13.78 carats.

Betsey Cushing was first married to James Roosevelt, son of U.S. President Franklin Delano Roosevelt. As her mother-in-law Eleanor Roosevelt did not like official or diplomatic entertaining, Betsey often used to act as hostess for her father in law, both at the White House and at Hyde Park, the Roosevelt family estate in up-state New York.

Betsey's marriage ended in 1942, whereupon she married Jock Hay Whitney, an even richer member of the monied American East Coast aristocracy. Together they collected extraordinary Impressionist pictures and Betsey was always on the best-dressed list. The Whitney Blue Diamond formed part of her estate, sold in 1998 at an auction in New York to benefit many philanthropic causes. It was one of a pair of pendant earrings, the other pendant being white.

After he bought the earrings, Graff re-polished the pear-shaped stones, which became respectively a vivid blue flawless of 10.64 carats and a white 'D' Flawless. The blue diamond was named the Whitney Blue by Graff; its accompanying 11.17-carat diamond he called the Whitney White. 'When I put in the winning bid,' Graff remembers, 'I knew I had the best blue diamond that existed in the world – it's a major, major stone and I later mounted it in a ring, which I kept for some years then sold at a price in excess of $10 million.'

Left: The Whitney Blue Diamond (10.64 carats) and the Whitney White Diamond (11.17 carats).
Above: Betsey and Jock Hay Whitney: Cecil Beaton/Corbis.

THE HARCOURT EMERALDS AND THE HARCOURT TIARA

The Harcourt emerald parure and tiara were wedding presents to Mary Hayes Burns from her mother, when she married Lewis, 1st Viscount Harcourt in 1899. Lady Harcourt's mother was a sister of J. Pierpont Morgan, the banker. The tiara was worn at the 1937 coronation of King George VI; and her daughter, Lady Ashburton, wore both the tiara and the parure at the 1953 coronation of The Queen. Both parure and tiara were composed of ancient and very beautiful step-cut emeralds, set within sprays of diamond flowerheads and ribbon motifs.

'I originally bought the magnificent parure some years ago,' Graff recollects. 'I broke it up and re-polished all the stones. When the tiara came up recently I bought that too, because it had a magnificent centre stone together with other top quality emeralds. I broke the tiara up as well, and re-polished all the stones. I am fascinated by the history of jewels, but I am more interested in the history of individual gems. If you think about it, the emeralds used for the necklace and the tiara probably came from an earlier piece of jewellery. Stones are always being recycled and given new leases of life. My challenge,' he says, 'is to acquire great gems and pass them on to my clients.'

Right: The Harcourt Tiara: Christie's.

Left: The Harcourt Emeralds: Christie's.
Above: The Harcourt Emeralds reset by Graff into a magnificent necklace.

MILLENNIUM

The Millennium necklace and the Paragon Diamond

For the 2000 Millennium celebrations, Graff created a truly magnificent Millennium necklace, formed of fancy intense blue, yellow and pink diamonds, from which was suspended an extraordinary diamond called the Paragon. This is a very unusual seven-sided stone, and at 137.82 carats was the world's largest 'D' Flawless diamond at the time. At a gala evening at Syon House, London, attended by H.R.H. The Prince of Wales, to celebrate the Millennium, the finale of the show featured Naomi Campbell, the supermodel, wearing this unique Graff piece.

Right: The Paragon Diamond (137.82 carats) suspended from the Millennium necklace.

THE GOLD AND THE YELLOW

**The Golden Drop Diamond, the Sarah Diamond,
the Golden Star Diamond, the Golden Maharajah Diamond,
the Rojtman Diamond, the Graff Vivid Yellow Diamond.**

The extraordinary Golden Drop Diamond is one of the most intense and pure yellow diamonds for its size, 18.31 carats, ever seen. By repute it was part of the collection of the rarest of coloured stones formed by the eccentric Duke of Brunswick. The Golden Drop is first recorded when it was in the possession of Louis Winans, one of those rare addicts of coloured diamonds who occur (like the Duke of Brunswick) throughout the history of the stones. The Winans family fortune had been made in railways in Russia in the mid-19th century and this quiet recluse had formed a superb collection of coloured diamonds.

Winans died in the mid-1920s and the collection was inherited by a female relation. It remained in her possession until she sold it at auction in the mid-1990s. During World War II, living in Brighton, she was concerned that Britain might be invaded, so she commissioned the local blacksmith to make an iron casket into which she put the Golden Drop and the other coloured diamonds and jewellery she had inherited. The casket was then buried in the garden and when the war was over it was still safely in the same location. After re-polishing and re-mounting the diamond in a ring, it was sold to a Hong Kong taipan for around $9 million.

The Sarah Diamond, cut by Laurence Graff in 2000, weighing 132.43 carats, is a lustrous, fancy vivid yellow cushion cut diamond, the largest ever known of its kind.

The Golden Maharajah is a wonderful golden-brown pear-shaped diamond of 65.57 carats, so very unusual that it has been widely exhibited during its history.

Right: The Golden Drop Diamond: 18.31 carats.

Above: The Golden Star Diamond: 101.28 carats.
Right: The Hope of Africa: 115.91 carats.

Originally belonging to a maharajah, it was exhibited in 1937 at the World's Fair in Paris where it attracted international attention. In 1939, and again in 1940, it was on exhibition at the New York World's Fair. In 1976 it was a star attraction at the opening of the Hall of Minerals and Gems at the Museum of Natural History in New York, where it was on loan from an anonymous New Yorker. There it remained until 1990. It was sold in 2006 to Graff.

The Rojtman Diamond is a fine cushion-shaped fancy yellow natural coloured diamond of 107.46 carats. Unusually, nothing is known of its history, prior to 1957 – however, it bears a resemblance to the 107.50-carat 'Star of Diamonds' found in the South African mines and mentioned by the jewellery historian Edwin Streeter in 1882. This was referred to by Louise Dieulafait, a 19th-century gem expert, as 'a lovely stone, which revealed under the microscope a prospect of pointed mountain crests, lit up by broad sunlight in all the colours of the rainbow.' Could these two stones be one and the same?

In 1957 the diamond was acquired by Mrs Marc Rojtman of New York, who then exhibited it at the Diamond Pavilion in Johannesburg in 1966. Later, it was acquired by Graff on one of his many visits to New York.

Right: The Rojtman Diamond: 107.46 carats.

'When I first saw the Graff Vivid Yellow Diamond in the rough,' Laurence Graff recalls, 'I was mesmerised by its unusual deep golden hue and I became entranced by its dream-like allure. It was as if it were on fire with flames of orange and sensational yellows which resembled a golden sun radiating glory and heat.' The rough diamond, of 190.7 carats, was of such an unusual and exceptional colour that it was sent to the Gemmological Institute of America for thorough testing to verify that it was entirely natural. It was. Now came the challenge of preserving the splendid colour of the stone alongside the magical weight of 100 carats. Graff's master cutter, Antonio Bianco, witnessed the heart-stopping moment when, after a period of nine months, he and his team realised the orange fire burning outside hid a 100.09-carat pure vivid yellow dream diamond of magnificent quality.

'It was truly the experience of a lifetime to see the Graff Vivid Yellow Diamond revealed in all its splendour for the first time,' says Graff, 'and one which is unlikely to be surpassed.'

Left: The Graff Vivid Yellow (100.09 carats) suspended from a 'D' Flawless pear-shaped diamond necklace.

GRAFF'S UNBORN DIAMONDS

The 15th largest rough diamond ever discovered is also the 10th largest white rough diamond, weighing 603 carats. Laurence Graff paid a record sum of over $12 million for it. The diamonds that will eventually emerge from this rough will have been studied for months on end before the first piece of this historic and huge stone is cleaved from its fellows. Only the future will witness the eventual jewellery delivered from this historic piece of diamond in the rough.

Graff does what he has always done: finding unique gems and dreaming up new and interesting ways of using them in the most fabulous jewels in the world.

Right: Laurence Graff in front of his portrait by Christoph Schellberg;
Andrey Bronnikov.
'Diamonds are a token of love. You can never have enough.'

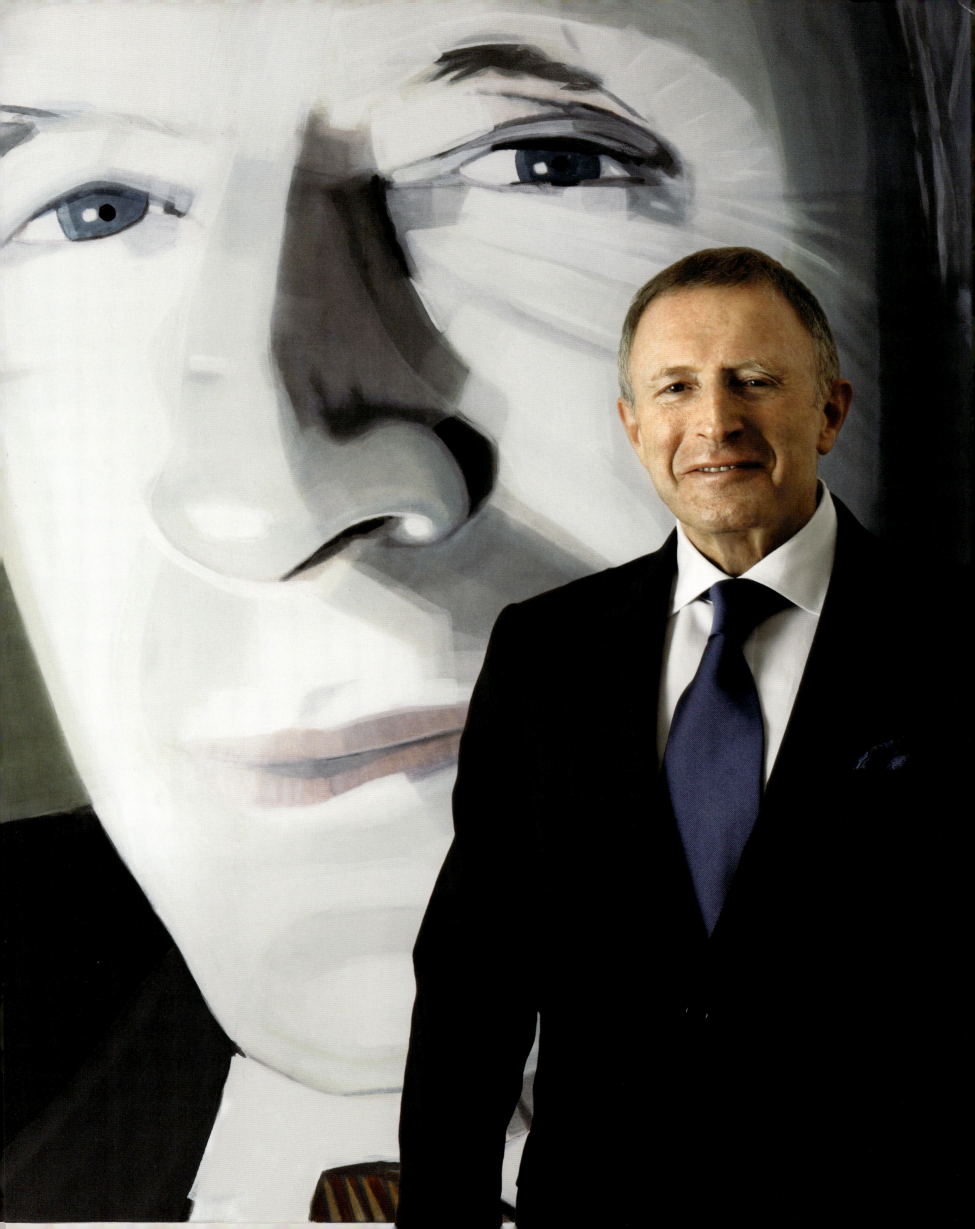

THE MOST FABULOUS JEWELS IN THE WORLD
by Meredith Etherington-Smith

Design: Anikst Design, London
Researcher: Emma Wright
For Graff: Gwen Keywood, Fiona Spence

Reproduction: DawkinsColour, Unichrome
Printed by: Graphicom, Italy

Published on behalf of Graff by:
Cultureshock Media, 27b Tradescant Road
London SW8 1DX

t. +44(0) 20 7735 9263
f. +44(0) 20 7735 5052
www.cultureshockmedia.co.uk
info@cultureshockmedia.co.uk

© Graff 2007

GRAFF
6-7 New Bond Street
London W1S 3SJ
T. +44 (0) 20 7584 8571

Distributed by Thames and Hudson outside North America
Thames and Hudson
181 High Holborn
London
United Kingdom
t. +44(0) 20 7845 5000
f. +44(0) 20 7845 5055
sales@thameshudson.co.uk

Distributed within North America by the Antique Collectors' Club Ltd. Antique Collectors' Club Ltd, Eastworks, 116 Pleasant Street, Suite 18, Easthampton, MA, 01027 USA

Every effort has been made to trace copyright holders and we apologise for any unintentional omission. A CIP record of this book is available from the British Library

All rights reserved. No part of this publication may be reproduced or transmitted in any form or by any means, electronic or mechanical, including photocopy, recording or any information storage or retrieval system, without permission in writing from the copyright owner.

ISBN 0-9546999-2-0
ISBN 978 0-9546999-2-5

Cover and back cover images: the Star of America Diamond, 100.57 carats